Joseph Moreau

Testimonials to the merits of Thomas Paine

Joseph Moreau

Testimonials to the merits of Thomas Paine

ISBN/EAN: 9783337281441

Printed in Europe, USA, Canada, Australia, Japan

Cover: Foto ©Andreas Hilbeck / pixelio.de

More available books at **www.hansebooks.com**

TESTIMONIALS

TO THE MERITS OF

THOMAS PAINE,

AUTHOR OF "COMMON SENSE," "THE CRISIS," "RIGHTS
OF MAN," "ENGLISH SYSTEM OF FINANCE,"
"AGE OF REASON," &C., &C.,

COMPILED BY

JOSEPH N. MOREAU.

"The World is my Country,
To do Good my Religion."—*Paine's Motto.*

BURLINGTON, N. J.: F. L. TAYLOR.
1861.

TO THE READER.

The following little work will, perhaps, give you a more high conception of the important and meritorious services of the "Archimedes of the Eighteenth Century" to mankind, than could be conceived from the perusal of any "Life" of him ever issued from the Press; for, instead of its being the opinion of one individual, and that opinion perhaps biased, it is a collection of the sentiments of some seventy Historians, Statesmen, Poets, and Divines, many of whom were opposed to his political, and almost all to his theological views. If it in the slightest degree adds to your appreciation of Paine, the object of the compiler will be accomplished.

JOSEPH N. MOREAU.

NOTE BY THE PUBLISHER.

MR. MOREAU, having joined the Pennsylvania Volunteers, left the work more incomplete than the publisher desired. In fact, it was exceedingly difficult, from the mass of testimony of like character to make selections of that which might be the most desirable for so small a work. Should Mr. Moreau return from the campaign, a similar pamphlet, containing the balance of testimonies, will doubtless be published.

TESTIMONIALS

TO THE MERITS OF

THOMAS PAINE.

———————●———————

GEN. GEORGE WASHINGTON,

First President of this great Republic, in a letter to Thomas Paine, inviting that author and patriot to partake with him, at Rocky-hill, says:—

"Your presence may remind Congress of your past services to this country, and if it is in my power to impress them, command my best exertions with freedom, as they will be rendered cheerfully, by one who entertains a lively sense of the importance of your works."

In his letter to Richard Henry Lee, of Virginia, this honored hero writes:—

"That his *Common Sense* and many of his *Crisis* were were well timed and had a happy effect upon the public mind, none I believe who will turn to the epoch at which they were published, will deny. That his services have hitherto passed off unnoticed is obvious to all."

Washington to Gen. Joseph Reed, March 1776:

"By private letters which I have lately received from Virginia, I find that "Common Sense" is working a pow. erful change there in the minds of many men."

"A few more such flaming arguments as were exhibited at Falmouth and Norfolk, added to the sound doctrine and unanswerable reasoning contained in the pamphlet " *Common Sense*," will not leave numbers at a loss to decide on the propriety of a separation."—*Gen. Washington, to Joseph Reed, dated Cambridge, Jan.* 31, 1776.

———

JOHN ADAMS,

The Second President of the United States, who spared no occasion to underrate Thomas Paine's services, and to assault his opinions and character, the transparent motive being a jealousy to be considered himself the greatest mover of the ball of Independence, thus writes to his wife on the 19th of March, 1776 :—

"You ask me what is thought of *Common Sense*. Sensible men think there are some whims, some sophisms, some artful addresses to superstitious notions, some keen attempt upon the passions, in this pamphlet. But all agree there is a great deal of good sense, delivered in clear, simple, concise and nervous style. His sentiments of the abilities of America, and of the difficulty of a reconciliation with Great Britain, are generally approved."

———

THOMAS JEFFERSON,

The third President of the United States, and the writer of the glorious "Declaration of Independence," thus speaks of the "Author Hero," who first suggested it, in a letter to Francis Eppes:

"You ask my opinion of Lord Bolingbroke and Thomas Paine. They were alike in making bitter enemies of the priests and pharisees of their day. Both were

honest men; both advocates for human liberty. * *
*' These two persons differed remarkably in the style
of their writing, each leaving a model of what is most
perfect in both extremes of the simple and the sublime.
No writer has exceeded Paine in ease and familiarity of
style, in perspicuity of expression, happiness of eluci-
dation, and in simple and unassuming language. In
this he may be compared with Dr. Franklin."

In 1801, in a letter to Paine tendering him a passage
to the United States from France, in a national vessel,
Jefferson writes:

"I am in hopes you will find us returned generally to
sentiments worthy of former times. In these it will be
your glory to have steadily labored, and with as much
effect as any man living. That you may long live to
continue your useful labors and to reap the reward of
the thankfulness of nations, is my sincere prayer."

JAMES MADISON,

The Fourth President of the United States, and ex-
pounder of the Constitution. In 1784, a bill was
brought before the Virginia Legislature, proposing to
give Mr. Paine a tract of land on the eastern shore of
Chesapeake Bay. It was defeated by a single vote.
Monroe stated that it would have been carried in his
favor, had he not written "Public Good." It was this
that called forth the following from Madison to Washington:

"Whether a greater disposition to reward patriotic
and distinguished exertions of genius will be found on
any succeeding occasion, is not for me to predetermine.
Should it finally appear that the merits of the man
whose writings have so much contributed to infuse and

foster the spirit of Independence in the people of America are unable to inspire them with a just beneficence, the world, it is to be feared, will give us as little credit for our policy as for our gratitude in this particular."

"I believe in one God, and no more; and I hope for happiness beyond this life. I believe in the equality of man; and I believe that religious duties consist in doing justice, loving mercy, and endeavoring to make our fellow creatures happy."—(*Thomas Paine. See "Age of Reason."*)

JAMES MONROE,

The fifth President of the United States. The following extract is from a letter written by this gentleman to Paine, previous to the release from the Luxembourg of "the Apostle of Liberty":

"It is necessary for me to tell you how much all your countrymen—I speak of the great mass of the people—are interested in your welfare. They have not forgotten the history of their own Revolution, and the difficult scenes through which they passed; nor do they review its several stages without reviving in their bosoms a due sensibility of the merits of those who served them in that great and arduous conflict. *The crime of ingratitude has not yet stained, and I hope never will stain our national character.* You are considered by them as not only having rendered important services in our own Revolution, but as being, on a more extensive scale, the friend of human rights, and a distinguished and able advocate in favor of public liberty. To the welfare of Thomas Paine the Americans are not, nor can they be, indifferent."

"It is unnatural and impolitic to admit men who would root up our independence to have any share in our legislation, either as electors or representatives, because the support of our independence rests, in a great measure, on the vigor and purity of our public bodies.—(*The Crisis, No.* 3.)

GEN. ANDREW JACKSON,

The "Hero of New Orleans," and the seventh President
of the United States, said to the venerable philanthropist, Judge Hertell, of New York, upon the latter
proposing the erection of a suitable monument to Thos.
Paine :

"Thomas Paine needs no monument made by hands;
he has erected himself a monument in the hearts of all
lovers of liberty. '*The Rights of Man,*' will be more
enduring than all the piles of marble or granite man
can erect."

THE REPUBLICANS AND REFORMERS

Of England, in 1792, looked upon Paine as the true
"Apostle of Freedom." They circulated a song to his
praise, commencing

"God save great Thomas Paine!
His *Rights of Man* proclaim
From pole to pole!"
(*See Preface, Cheetham's Life of Paine.*)

" To argue with a man who has renounced the use and authority
of reason, and whose philosophy consists in holding humanity in
contempt, is like administering medicine to the dead, or endeavoring to convert an Atheist with Scripture."—(*The Crisis, No.* 5.)

BENJAMIN FRANKLIN,

Who first introduced Thomas Paine to the new world,
says, in a letter he gave the English Exciseman recom-
mending him to his son-in-law, Richard Bache (1774)

" The bearer, Mr. Thomas Paine, is very well recommended to me as an ingenious, worthy young man. He

goes to Pennsylvania with a view of settling there. I
request you to give him your best advice and counte-
nance."

About 13 years after, Dr. Franklin gave him letters
of introduction to several of the most prominent of the
French "men of letters." The following is an extract
from one to the Duc de la Rochefoucauld:

"The bearer of this is Mr. Paine, the author of a
famous piece entitled *Common Sense*, published here with
great effect on the minds of the people at the beginning
of the Revolution. He is an ingenious, honest man;
and as such I beg leave to recommend him to your
civilities."

TIMOTHY PITKINS,

In his Political and Civil History of the United States,
says:—"Common Sense" produced a wonderful effect
in the different Colonies in favor of Independence.

REV. SOLOMON SOUTHWICK,

Printer, politician and lecturer against Infidelity, and,
at one time, the editor and publisher of *The Christian
Visiter,* says:

"No page in history, stained as it is with treachery
and falsehood, or cold-blooded indifference to right or
wrong, exhibits a more disgraceful instance of public
ingratitude than that which Thomas Paine experienced
from an age and country which he had so faithfully
served. As the Tintochus of the Revolution, and it is
no exaggeration to style him such, we owe everlasting
gratitude to his name and memory. Why, then, was

he suffered to sink into the most wretched poverty and obscurity, after having, in both hemispheres, so signally distinguished himself as the friend of liberty and mankind? Was his religion, or want of religion, the real or affected cause? Did not those who feared his talents, make his religion a pretext not only to treat him with cold neglect, but to strip him, if possible, of every laurel he had won in the political field, *as the brilliant, undaunted and successful* advocate of freedom? As to his religion, or no religion, God alone must be the judge and arbiter of that. No human being, no human tribunal, can claim a right even to censure him for it, much less to make it the pretext for defrauding him, either in life or death, of the reward due to his patriotism, or the legitimate fame of his exertions in the cause of suffering humanity. Had Thomas Paine been guilty of any crime, we should be the last to eulogize his memory. But we cannot find he ever was guilty of any other crime than that of advancing his opinions freely upon all subjects connected with public liberty and happiness. If he erred in any of his opinions, since we know that his intentions were pure, we are bound to cover his errors with the mantle of charity. We cannot say here all that we would wish to say. A brief note is insufficient to do justice to so important a subject. We may, however, safely affirm that Paine's conduct in America was that of a real patriot. In the French Convention he displayed the same pure and disinterested spirit; there his humanity shone forth in his exertions to save, at the risk of his own life, the unfortunate Louis XVI from the scaffold. His life, it is true, was written by a ministerial hireling, who strove in vain to blacken his moral character. The late James Cheetham, likewise, wrote his life; and we have no hesitation in saying, that we knew perfectly

2

well at the time the motives of that author for writing and publishing a work which, we have every reason to believe, is a libel almost from beginning to end. In fact, Cheetham had become tired of this country, and had formed a plan to return to England and become a ministerial editor, in opposition to Cobbett, and his "Life of Paine" was written to pave his way back again. We, therefore, presume that he acted upon the principle that the end justified the means. * * * *
Had Thomas Paine been a Grecian or Roman patriot, in olden times, and performed the same public services as he did for this country, he would have had the honor of an Apotheosis. The Pantheon would have been opened to him, and we should at this day regard his memory with the same veneration that we do that of Socrates and Cicero. But posterity will do him justice: Time, that destroys envy and establishes truth, will clothe his character in the habiliments that justly belong to it. * * * *   We cannot resist the disposition to say, that in suffering the home of the author of "Common Sense," "The Crisis," and "The Rights of Man," to lie neglected, in the first place; and secondly, in permitting it to be violated, and his bones shipped off to a foreign country, contrary to all the laws of decency and civilization, we have added nothing to the justice or dignity of our national character; and we shall rejoice if impartial history tax us not with a gross departure from both."

"The key of heaven is not in the keeping of any sect, nor ought the road to it to be obstructed by any. Our relation to each other in this world is as men, and the man who is a friend to man and to his rights, let his religious opinions be what they may, is a good citizen, to whom I can give, as I ought to do, and as every other ought, the right hand of fellowship."—(*Paine's Letter to Samuel Adams, Jan.* 1, 1808.)

DR. BENJAMIN RUSH,

A member from Philadelphia of the Continental Congress, and Signer of the Declaration of Independence, gives the following account of the first appearance of "Common Sense":

"At that time there was a certain Robert Bell, an intelligent Scotch printer and bookseller of Philadelphia, whom I knew to be as high-toned as Mr. Paine upon the subject of Independence. I mentioned the pamphlet to him, and he at once consented to run the risk of publishing it. The author and the printer were immediately brought together, and 'Common Sense' bursted from the press of the latter, in a few days, with an effect which has rarely been produced by types and paper in any age or country."

"Mr. Paine's manner of life was desultory. He often visited in the families of Dr. Franklin, Mr. Rittenhouse, and Mr. George Clymer, where he made himself acceptable by a turn he discovered for philosophical as well as political subjects."

————

"He (Paine) contributed much in aid of the Revolution by publishing a pamphlet entitled 'Common Sense.'"— (*Duganne's Comprehensive Summary.*)

————

RICHARD HENRY LEE,

A distinguished patriot of the Revolution, and who, as member of Congress from Virginia, in 1776, first proposed to that body the Declaration of Independence, in returning thanks to General Washington for a copy of the *Rights of Man*, remarked:

"It is a performance of which any man might be proud; and I most sincerely regret that our country could not have offered sufficient inducements to have retained, as a permanent citizen, a man so thoroughly republican in sentiment, and fearless in the expression of his opinion."

In a letter of Lee to WASHINGTON, dated Chantilly, 22d July, 1784, he says:

"The very great respect that I shall ever pay to your recommendations, would have been very sufficient to have procured my exertions in favor of Mr. Paine, independent of his great public merits in our Revolution. I have a perfect knowledge of the extraordinary effects produced by that gentleman's writings; effects of such an important nature as would render it very unworthy of these States to let him suffer anywhere; but it would be culpable indeed to permit it under their own eye, and within their own limits. I had not the good fortune to be present when Mr. Paine's business was considered in the House of Delegates (of Virginia) or, most certainly, I should have exerted myself in his behalf. I have been told that a proposition in his favor has miscarried, from its being observed that he had shown enmity to the State by having written a pamphlet (The Public Good) injurious to our claim of Western territory. It has ever appeared to me that this pamphlet was the consequence of Mr. Paine's being himself imposed upon; and that it was rather the fault of the place than of the man. This, however, was but a trifle, when compared with the great and essential services that his other writings have done for the United States."

"It is the duty of every man, as far as his ability extends, to detect and expose delusion and error. But nature has not given to every one a talent for the purpose; and among those to whom such talent is given, there is often a want of disposition or of courage to do it."—(*Paine's Examination of Testament.*)

NAPOLEON BONAPARTE.

The following is related by Clio Rickman, the Poet, who was with Paine in France:

"When Bonaparte returned (to Paris) from Italy, he called on Mr. Paine and invited him to dinner. In the course of his rapturous address to him, he declared that a statue of gold ought to be erected to him in every city of the universe, assuring him that he always slept with his book "Rights of Man" under his pillow, and conjured him to honor him with his correspondence and advice."

Rickman then remarks on the above:

"This anecdote is only related as a *fact;* of the sincerity of the compliment those must judge who know Bonaparte's principles best."

It might be here added, that when Napoleon meditated his invasion of England, by means of gunboats, he secured the services of Paine to organize a government if it proved successful.

"Paine was in Washington's camp in December, 1776, and the first number of the 'Crisis' was published. It was read to every Corporal's guard, and its strong and truthful language had a powerful effect in the army and among the people at large."—*Benj. F. Lossing, in his Field Book of the Revolution, vol. 2, p. 275, Note.*

MAJOR-GENERAL CHARLES LEE,

Fourteen days after the publication of "Common Sense," thus wrote to General Washington:

"Have you seen the pamphlet 'Common Sense?' I never saw such a masterly, irresistible performance. It will, if I mistake not, in concurrence with the transcendent folly and wickedness of the ministry, give the *coup*

2*

de grace to Great Britain. In short, I own myself convinced by the arguments of the necessity of separation." General Lee, speaking of the wonderful effects of Paine's writings, said, that "He burst forth on the world like Jove in thunder!" John Adams says that Lee used to speak of Paine as "the man with genius in his eyes."

WILLIAM MASSEY,

In his History of England, says: "Thomas Paine's pamphlet, *Common Sense*, in which the new doctrines of liberty and equality were broadly taught, was published in America, in January, 1776, and had an immense circulation."

Extract from a letter from a gentleman in Charleston, S. C., dated February 14, 1776:

"Who is the author of *Common Sense?* I can hardly refrain from adoring him. He deserves a statue of gold."—*Pennsylvania Journal, March* 27, 1776.

CHARLES WILSON PEALE,

In a letter to Silas Deane, dated Philadelphia, July 28, 1779, says:

"Believing Mr. Paine to be a firm friend to America, and by personal acquaintance with him, gives me an opportunity of knowing that he had done more for our common cause than the world, who had *only seen* his publications, could know, I thought it my duty to support him."

AARON BURR,

In his compendium of the "Life of Paine," (New York, 1837) Gilbert Vale says:

"In reply to a query which we recently put to Col. Burr, as to Mr. Paine's alleged vulgarity, intemperance and want of cleanliness, as disseminated by those who wished it true, he remarked with dignity, '*Sir, he dined at my table.*' Then, am I to understand he was a gentleman? 'Certainly, sir,' replied Col. Burr, 'I always considered Mr. Paine a gentleman, a pleasant companion, and a good-natured and intelligent man, decidedly temperate, with a proper regard to his personal appearance, whenever I saw him.'"

JUDGE COOPER,

Who was, according to Thomas Jefferson, " One of the ablest men in America, and that in several branches of science," thus wrote :

" I was at Paris at this time (1792,) but previous to my going there, Mr. Paine, whom I had met at Mr. Johnson's, my bookseller, in St Paul's Churchyard, gave me letters of introduction to M. DeCondorcet, and his wife, Madame DeCondorcet, who read and spoke the English language with considerable facility. These letters introduced me to the interesting society of that very talented writer and his family. I found the letters of introduction of Mr. Paine honored with that attention which might be expected towards an estimable and distinguished man. * ,* * * I have dined with Mr. Paine in literary society, at Mr. Tiffins', a merchant in London, at least a dozen times, when his dress, manners, and conversation were such as became the character of an unobtrusive, intelligent gentleman, accustomed to good society. * * * Paine's opinions on theological topics underwent no change before his death."

HENRY C. WRIGHT

Says :—"Thomas Paine had a clear idea of God. This Being embodied his highest conception of truth, love, wisdom, mercy, liberty and power."

REV. M. D. CONWAY,

In a Sermon preached in Cincinnati, Ohio, on the 29th of January, 1860, said:

"All efforts to stain the good name of Thomas Paine have recoiled on those who made them, like poisoned arrows shot against a strong wind. * * * In his life, in his justice, in his truth, in his adherence to high principles, in his disinterestedness, I look in vain for his parallel in those times, and in these times. I am selecting my words; I know I am to be held accountable for them. So disinterested was he, that when his works were printed by the ten thousand, and as fast as one edition was out another was demanded, he, a poor and pinched author, who might very easily have grown rich, would not accept one cent for them, declared that he would not coin his principles, and made to the States a present of the copyrights. His brain was his fortune— nay, his living; he gave it all to American Independence."

"I trouble not myself about the manner of future existence. I content myself with believing, even to positive conviction, that the power that gave me existence is able to continue it in any form and manner he pleases, either with or without this body; and it appears more probable to me that I shall continue to exist hereafter, than that I should have had existence as I now have before that existence began."—(*Paine's Age of Reason, page* 57, *Philada. ed.*)

THOMAS CAMPBELL,

The Poet, whose lyrics and didactic writings have secured him a niche in the Temple of Fame, says:

"Those who remember the impression that was made by Burke's writings on the then living generation, will recollect that in the better educated classes of society there was a general proneness to go with Burke, and it is my sincere opinion that that proneness would have become universal, if such a mind as Mackintosh's had not presented itself, like a break-water to the general spring-tide of Burkeism. I may be reminded there was such a man as Thomas Paine, and that he strongly answered at the bar of public opinion all the arguments of Burke. I do not deny this fact; and I should be sorry if I could be blind, even with tears for Mackintosh in my eyes, to the services that have been rendered to the cause of truth by the shrewdness and courage of Thomas Paine. But without disparagement to Paine, in a great and essential view, it must be admitted that, though radically sound in sense, he was deficient in the strategetics of philosophy; whilst Mackintosh met Burke perfectly his equal in the tactics of moral science and in beauty of style and illustration. Hence Mackintosh went as the apostle of liberalism among a class, perhaps too influential in society, to whom the manners of Paine was repulsive."

EDMUND BURKE,

The celebrated Statesman and Orator, whose "Reflections on the French Revolution" called forth the "Rights of Man," speaks of "Common Sense" as "that celebrated pamphlet which *prepared* the minds of the people for Independence."

RAMSAY,

Who, like Gordon, was cotemporary with Paine, says, in his "History of the Revolution," alluding to "*Common Sense,*" (see vol. 1, pp. 336–7, London 1793.)

"In union with the feelings and sentiments of the people, it produced surprising effects. Many thousands were convinced, and were led to approve and long for a separation from the Mother Country; though that measure, a few months before, was not only foreign to their wishes, but the object of their abhorrence, the current suddenly became so strong in its favor, that it bore down all before it."

"Let each of us hold out to his neighbor the hearty hand of friendship, and unite in drawing a line, which, like an act of oblivion, shall bury in forgetfulness every former dissension: Let the names of Whig and Tory be extinct, and let none other be heard among us than those of a virtuous supporter of the RIGHTS OF MANKIND, and of the FREE AND INDEPENDENT STATES OF AMERICA."—(*Conclusion of Common Sense.*)

LORD EDWARD FITZGERALD,

The noble, but unfortunate, Irish patriot, thus wrote to his mother, from Paris, in 1792, of the abused Thomas Paine, showing clearly that the more closely the habits

of that great man were studied, the more great and re-
splendent did. they shine forth:

"I lodge with my friend Paine; we breakfast, dine
and sup together. The more I see of his interior, the
more I like and respect him. I cannot express how
kind he has been to me; there is a simplicity of manner, a goodness of heart, and a strength of mind in him
that I NEVER KNEW A MAN BEFORE POSSESS."

. WILLIAM GRIMSHAW,

In his "History of the United States," after acknow-
ledging the merits of Dickinson, Bland, Franklin,
Nicholas, Lee, Jefferson, and others, who supported the
cause of the colonists with their pens, says:

"But the most powerful writer was the celebrated
Thomas Paine, of London, who resided for some time in
America, and, in a work entitled *Common Sense*, roused
the public feeling to a degree unequaled by any previous
appeal."

MARQUIS DE CHASTELLEUX,

Author of a work on " Public Happiness" and a cherished
friend of General Washington, thus speaks of Paine, in
his " Travels in America :"

" I know not how it happened that since my arrival
in America, I had not yet seen Mr. Paine, that author
so celebrated in America and throughout Europe, by his
excellent work entitled, 'Common Sense,' and several
other political pamphlets. M. De Lafayette and myself had asked the permission of an interview for the
14th, in the morning, and we waited on him accordingly
with Col. Laurens. I discovered at his apartments all

the attributes of a man of letters, a room pretty much in disorder, dusty furniture, and a large table covered with books, lying open, and manuscripts begun. * * Having formerly held a post in Government, he has now no connection with it; and as his patriotism and his talents are unquestionable, it is natural to conclude that the vivacity of his imagination, and the independence of his character, render him more calculated for reasoning on affairs, than for conducting them."

" The ' Rights of Man' had much been read in this country. Even the ' Age of Reason' had obtained an immense circulation from the great reputation of the author."—(Atlantic Monthly, vol. 4, p. 9.)

LORD ERSKINE,

"The greatest forensic advocate since the days of Cicero," speaking of the American Revolution, said:

"In that great and calamitous conflict, Edmund Burke and Thomas Paine fought in the same field together, but with very different success. Mr. Burke spoke to a Parliament in England, such as Sir George Saville describes it, having no ears but for sounds that flattered its corruptions. Mr. Paine, on the other hand, spoke to the people, reasoned with them, told them they were bound by no subjection to any sovereignty, further than their own benefit connected them; and by these powerful arguments *prepared* the minds of the American people for that glorious, just, and happy Revolution."

JUDGE HERTELL,

Of New York, says:

"No man in modern ages has done more to benefit mankind, or distinguished himself more for the immense moral good he has effected for his species than Thomas Paine; who in truth merits eternal life, and, doubtless will be immortalized in the memory and gratitude of future generations of happy beings, who will continue to hymn his praises and make his merits known to remotest posterity."

"It was the cause of America that made me an author."—(*Thos. Paine.*)

SIR FRANCIS BURDETT

Thus alluded to Thomas Paine, in a speech in London, in 1797, as Chairman of a meeting of the "Friends of Parliamentary Reform":

"Union! It is union among the people that ministers dread. They are aware that when once the people unite in demanding their rights, then there must be an end to illegitimate power; I mean all power not derived from the people. Ministers know that a united people are not to be resisted; and it is this that we must understand by what is written in the works of an *honest man too long calumniated*, I mean Thomas Paine."

MADAME DE STAEL,

In her "Considerations on the French Revolution," says:

"Thomas Paine was the most violent of the American Democrats; and yet, there was neither calculation nor hypocrisy in his political exaggerations. When the sentence of Louis XVI came under discussion, he alone advised what would have done honor to France if it had

3

been adopted, the offer to the King of an asylum in America. 'The Americans are grateful to him,' said Paine, 'for having promoted their Independence.'"

MADAME ROLAND,

In her "Appeal," says: (See vol. i, part 2, page 45, ed. 1798.)

"Among the persons I was in the habit of receiving, and of whom I have already described the most remarkable, Paine deserves to be mentioned. Declared a French citizen, as one of those celebrated foreigners whom the nation ought with eagerness to adopt, he was known by writings which had been useful in the American Revolution, and might have contributed to produce one in England. I shall not take upon me to decide decisively on his character, because he understood French without speaking it, and I was nearly in the same situation with respect to English; I was, therefore, less able to converse with him myself than to listen to his discourses with those whose political talents were greater than my own. The boldness of his conceptions, the originality of his style, the striking truths which he boldly throws out in the midst of those whom they offend, must necessarily have produced great effects; but I should think him better qualified to scatter, if I may be allowed the expression, the flames of conflagration, than to discuss primary principles or prepare the formation of Government."

GENERAL WASHINGTON'S ALLOWANCE OF GROG TO HIS GARDENER.—G. W. P. Custis, in his "Recollections of Washington," gives a copy of a contract, written in Washington's own hand, between George Washington and Philip Barton, his gardener. After the usual clauses, it provides that the said Barton "will not, at any time, suffer himself to be disguised with liquor, except on terms hereafter mentioned." After enumerating the clothing, etc., to be furnished, it further says, he was to be allowed "four dollars at Christmas, with which he may be drunk four days and four nights. Also, two dollars at Whitsuntide to be drunk two days; also a dram in the morning, and a drink of grog at dinner at noon."

REV. GEORGE CROLY,

In his "Life of George IV," thus speaks of Thomas Paine:

"An impartial estimate of this remarkable person has been rarely formed, and still more rarely expressed. He was, assuredly, one of the original men of the age in which he lived. It has been said that he owed success to vulgarity. No one competent to judge, could read a page of his 'Rights of Man,' without seeing that this is a clumsy misrepresentation. There is a peculiar originality in his style of thought and expression, his diction is not vulgar or illiterate, but nervous, simple, and scientific. Others have said of him, with more truth, that he owed his popularity to the hardihood with which he proclaimed and vindicated his errors. Paine, like the young Spartan warrior, went into the field stripped bare to the last thread of prudent conventional disguise; and thus not only fixed the gaze of men upon his intrepid singularity, but exhibited the vigor of his faculties in full play. His ambition seems to have been that of an eccentric, well-intentioned desperado."

"I consider myself in the hands of my Creator, and that he will dispose of me after this life consistently with his justice and goodness. I leave all these matters to Him as my Creator and friend, and I hold it to be presumption in man to make an article of faith as to what the Creator will do with us hereafter."—(*Thos. Paine's* "*Thoughts on a Future State.*")

"Though Nature is gay, polite, and generous abroad, she is sullen, rude and niggardly at home: return the visit and she admits you with all the suspicion of a miser, and all the reluctance of an antiquated beauty retired to replenish her charms. Bred up in antediluvian notions, she has not yet acquired the European taste of receiving visitants in her dressing-room; she locks and bolts up her private recesses with extraordinary care, as if not only resolved to preserve her hoards but to conceal her age, and hide the remains of a face that was young and lovely in the days of Adam. He that would view Nature in her undress, and partake of her internal treasures, must proceed with the resolution of a robber, if not a ravisher. She gives no invitation to follow her to the cavern. The external earth makes no proclamation of the interior stores, but leaves to chance and industry the discovery of the whole. In such gifts as nature can annually re-create, she is noble and profuse, and entertains the whole world with the interests of her fortunes, but watches over the capital with the care of a miser. Her gold and jewels lie concealed in the earth, in caves of utter darkness; the hoards of wealth, heaps upon heaps, mould in the chests, like the riches of a necromancer's cell. It must be very pleasant to an adventurous speculist to make excursions into these Gothic regions; and in his travels he may possibly come to a cabinet locked up in some rocky vault, whose treasures shall reward his toil, and enable him to shine, on his return, as splendidly as nature herself."—(*Written by Paine for the "Pennsylvania Magazine."*)

JOEL BARLOW,

The poet, patriot and statesman, an intimate friend of Paine, says:

"He was one of the most benevolent and disinterested of mankind, endowed with the clearest perception, an uncommon share of original genius, and the greatest depth of thought. * * * *

"He ought to be ranked among the brightest and undeviating luminaries of the age in which he lived.

"As a visiting acquaintance and a literary friend, he was one of the most instructive men I ever have known.

He had a surprising memory and a brilliant fancy. His mind was a storehouse of facts and useful observations. He was full of lively anecdote, and ingenious, original, pertinent remark upon almost every subject. *. * *

"He was always charitable to the poor beyond his means, a sure protector and a friend to all Americans in distress that he found in foreign countries; and he had frequent occasion to exert his influence in protecting them during the Revolution in France. * * *

"His writings will answer for his patriotism." * *

"In a great affair, where the good of man is at stake, I love to work for nothing; and so fully am I under the influence of this principle, that I should lose the spirit, the pleasure, and the pride of it, were I conscious that I looked for reward.—(*Thomas Paine.*)

R. SHELTON MACKENZIE, D. C. L.,

An author, critic and literary editor of great ability, in an article on Muir, the Scotch Reformer, published in the Philadelphia *Press*, said:

"Holding the belief that Paine's theological works had much better never have been written, we cannot ignore the fact that he was one of the ablest politicians of his time, and that liberal minds, all over the world, recognized him as such. The publication of his 'Rights of Man,' while the French Revolution was proceeding, had so greatly alarmed Pitt, and the other members of the British Government, that a state prosecution was commenced to crush himself and his book."

REV. JEDEDIAH MORSE,

In his "Annals of the American Revolution," says:

"A pamphlet, under the signature of 'Common Sense,' written by Thomas Paine, produced a great effect.
3*

While it demonstrates the necessity, the advantages, and the practicability of Independence, it treats kingly government with opprobrium, and hereditary succession with ridicule. The change of the public mind on this occasion *is without a parallel.*"

"Those who expect to reap the blessings of freedom, must, like men, undergo the fatigues of supporting it. We fight not to enslave, but to set a country free."—(*The Crisis, No.* 4.)

WILLIAM COBBETT,

Author of a "History of the Reformation," and several other works, and at one time a violent opponent of Thos. Paine, says, in his "Paper against Gold":

"In principles of finance, Mr. Paine was deeply skilled; and to his very great and rare talents as a writer, he added an uncommon degree of experience in the concerns of paper money. * * * Events have proved the truths of his principles on this subject, and to point out the fact is no more than an act of justice due to his talents, and an act more particularly due at my hands, *I having been one of his most violent assailants.*"

In his "Political Register," he confessed that,

"Old age having laid his hand upon this truly great man, this truly philosophical politician, at his expiring flambeau I lighted my taper."

He also says:

"I saw Paine *first pointing the way,* and then *leading* a nation through perils and difficulties of all sorts to INDEPENDENCE, and to lasting liberty, prosperity, and greatness."

"The word of God is the creation we behold: and it is in this word, which no human invention can counterfeit or alter, that God speaketh universally to man."—(*Thos. Paine's Age of Reason, p.* 25, *Philadelphia edition.*)

ABBE SIEYES,

The distinguished French statesman, in 1791, upon the appearance of Paine's "Rights of Man" in France, thus wrote:

"Mr. Thomas Paine is one of those men who most contributed to the establishment of a Republic in America. In England, his ardent love of humanity, and his hatred of every form of tyranny, prompted him to defend the French Revolution against the rhapsodical declamation of Mr. Burke. His ' Rights of Man,' translated into our language, is universally known, and where is the patriotic Frenchman who has not already, from the depths of his soul, thanked him for having fortified our cause with all the power of his reason and his reputation. It is with great pleasure that I embrace this occasion to offer him a tribute of my thankfulness and profound esteem, for the truly philanthrophic use he makes of his distinguished talents."

SAMUEL ADAMS,

One of the most bold and sturdy patriots of the revolution, and a signer of the Declaration of Independence, in 1802, in a letter to Paine, lamenting the publication of the " Age of Reason," says:

"I have frequently, with pleasure, reflected on your services to my native and your adopted country. Your 'Common Sense,' and your 'Crisis' unquestionably awakened the public mind, and led the people loudly to call for a Declaration of our National Independence."

ARTHUR O'CONNER

Wrote the following lines, had them printed, and distributed them himself, on his way to imprisonment at Fort George, in 1798:

I.

" The pomp of courts and pride of kings,
 I prize beyond all earthly things;
 I love my country,—but the king,
 Above all men, his praise I sing;
 The royal banners are displayed
 And may success the standard aid.

II.

" I fain would banish far from hence
 The *Rights of Man* and *Common Sense*,
 Confusion to his odious reign,
 That foe to princes—Thomas Paine!
 Defeat and Ruin seize the cause
 Of France, her liberties and laws."

(Read the first line of the second verse immediately after the first line of the first verse—the second line of the second verse, after the second line of the first, and thus continue throughout to connect the corresponding lines of each verse—having previously read them in the usual manner. The two modes of reading will be found ingeniously to convey distinct and opposite meanings.)

———

An American girl once observed of Mr Paine, that, " His head was like an orange—it had a separate apartment for everything it contained."

WILLIAM HOWITT,

In " Cassell's Illustrated History of England," says :

" There was no man in the Colonies, nevertheless, who contributed so much to bring the open Declaration of Independence to a crisis, as Thomas Paine, the celebrated author of ' The Rights of Man,' and the ' Age of Reason.' " * * *

" This Pamphlet (Common Sense) was the spark which was all that was needed to fire the train of Independence. It at once seized on the imagination of the public; cast all other writers into the shade, and flew in thousands and tens of thousands all over the Colonies. * * * During the winter and spring, this lucid and admirably reasoned pamphlet was read and discussed everywhere, and by all classes, bringing the conviction that immediate independence was necessary. The common fire blazed up in the Congress, and the thing was done. * * * * He (Paine) became the great oracle on subjects of governments and constitutions, and contrived, both by personal exertions and through the press, to urge on the utter separation of the Colonies from the mother country."

" Ship Building is America's greatest pride, in which, she will, in time, excel the whole world."—(*Paine's " Common Sense.*")   .

MARY HOWITT,

In her "History of the United States," says:

"Early in this year (1776) Thomas Paine, a recent emigrant to America, and editor of the *Pennsylvania Magazine*, published a pamphlet, called 'Common Sense,' which spoke at once the secret sentiment of the people. It went direct to the point, showing, in the simplest but strongest language, the folly of keeping up the British connection, and the absolute necessity which existed for separation. The cause of Independence took, as it were, a definite form from this moment."

HON. SALMA HALE,

In his "History of the United States," says:

"A pamphlet, entitled 'Common Sense,' written by Mr. Thomas Paine, an Englishman, was universally read, and most highly admired. In language plain, forcible, and singularly well fitted to operate on the public mind, he portrayed the excellencies of Republican institutions, and attacked, with happy and successful ridicule, the principles of hereditary government. The effect of the pamphlet in making converts was astonishing, and is probably without precedent in the annals of literature."

CHARLES JAMES FOX,

The English statesman, said of Paine's 'Rights of Man:'

"It seems as clear and as simple as the first rule of arithmetic."

MARY L. BOOTH,

In her excellent "History of New York," alluding to the opposition to Independence manifested by the masses in the early part of the struggle, says:

"At this juncture 'Common Sense' was published in Philadelphia, by Thomas Paine, and electrified the whole nation with the spirit of Independence and Liberty. This eloquent production *severed the last link* that bound the Colonies to the mother country; it boldly gave speech to the arguments which had long been trembling on the lips of many, but which none before had found courage to utter; and, *accepting its conclusions,* several of the Colonies instructed their delegates, in the Continental Congress, to close their eyes against the *ignis fatuus* of loyalty, and fearlessly to throw off their allegiance to the Crown."

REV. WILLIAM GORDON,

In his "History of the Revolution," says: (vol. 2, p. 78, New York, 1794.)

"The publications which have appeared have greatly promoted the spirit of Independency, but no one so much as the pamphlet under the signature of ' Common Sense,' written by Mr. Thomas Paine, an Englishman. Nothing could have been better timed than this performance. It has produced most astonishing effects."

GEN. WM. A. STOKES,

A distinguished member of the Bar of Pennsylvania, and by no means an admirer of Paine, is obliged, like Cheetham, to confess that the author of " Common Sense" and the " Crisis"

" Eagerly embraced the cause of the Colonies, and was soon to act an important and meritorious part. When ' Common Sense' was published a great blow was struck—it was felt from New England to the Carolinas, it resounded throughout the world. * * * * He not only reasoned, he flattered ; he availed himself of prejudice, he dealt freely in invective. For this I do not censure him; for the TRIBUNE OF THE PEOPLE, WHOSE WORDS

WERE TO DISMEMBER AN EMPIRE, might well resort to all the aïds of art in accomplishing his stupendous task. * * * * Paine's brawny arm applied the torch which set the country in a flame, to be extinguished only by the relinquishment of British supremacy, and for *this*, irrespective of his motives and character, HE MERITS THE GRATITUDE OF EVERY AMERICAN."

SAMUEL BRYAN,

Secretary to Council of Censors on Pennsylvania Constitution, 1776, said:

"This book, 'Common Sense,' may be called the book of Genesis, for it was the beginning. From this book sprang the Declaration of Independence, that not only laid the foundation of liberty in our own country, but the good of mankind throughout the world."

CHARLES PHILLIPS,

The eloquent Irish barrister, wrote the following beautiful tribute to Paine. It may be found in his "Loves of Celestine and St. Hubert:"

"Among these, there was one whom I could not help viewing with peculiar admiration, because, by the sole power of surprising genius, he had surmounted the disadvantages of birth and the difficulties of fortune. It was the celebrated Thomas Paine, a man who, no matter what may be the difference of opinion as to his principles, must ever remain a proud example of mind, unpatronized and unsupported, eclipsing the factitious beams of rank, and wealth, and pedigree! I never saw him in his captivity, or heard the revilings by which he has since been assailed, without cursing in my heart that ungenerous feeling which, cold to the necessities of genius, is clamorous in the publication of its defects. * * * * 'Ye great ones of his nation! ye pretended moralists, so forward now to cast your *interested* indignation upon the memory of Paine, where were you in the day of his adversity? which of you, to assist his infant merit, would diminish even the surplus of your debaucheries? where the mitred charity—the practical religion? Consistent declaimers, rail on! What, though his genius was the gift of heaven, his heart the altar of friendship! What, though wit and eloquence, and anecdote flowed freely from his tongue, while conviction made her voice his messenger! What, though thrones trembled, and prejudice fled, and freedom came at his command! He dared to question the creed which you, believing, contradicted, and to despise the rank which you, boasting of, debased.'"

PAUL ALLEN,

In his "History of the American Revolution," says:

"Among the numerous writers on this momentous question, the most luminous, the most eloquent, and the most forcible, was Thomas Paine. His pamphlet, entitled 'Common Sense,' was not only read, but understood, by everybody. It contained plain and simple truths, told in a style and language that came home to the heart of every man; and those who regard the independence of the United States as a blessing, will never cease to cherish the remembrance of Thomas Paine. Whatever may have been his subsequent career—in whatever light his moral or religious principles may be regarded, it should never be forgotten that to him, more than to any single individual, was owing the rapid diffusion of those sentiments and feelings which produced the act of separation from Great Britain."

4

ROBERT BISSET, LL.D.,

In his "Life of Edmund Burke," says:

"A pamphlet, entitled 'Common Sense,' published by Thomas Paine, afterwards so famous in Europe, contributed very much to the ratification of the independence of America." * * *

In his "History of the Reign of George III," Bisset says:

"Thomas Paine was represented (in England) as the minister of God, diffusing light to a darkened world."

RICHARD HILDRETH,

In his "History of the United States," says:

"No little excitement was produced by the publication, in Philadelphia, about this time, (1776) of 'Common Sense,' a pamphlet by Thomas Paine. * * * * It argued in that plain and convincing style, for which Paine was so distinguished, the folly of any longer attempting to keep up the British connection, and the absolute necessity of a final and formal separation. Pitched exactly to the popular tone, it had a wide circulation throughout the Colonies, and gave a powerful impulse to the cause of independence."

THOMAS CLIO RICKMAN,

Author of a number of poems, tales and political pamphlets, says:

"Why seek occasions, surly critics and detractors, to maltreat and misrepresent Mr. Paine? He was mild, unoffending, sincere, gentle, humble, and unassuming;

his talents were soaring, acute, profound, extensive and original; and he possessed that charity which covers a multitude of sins."

"I ever feel myself hurt when I hear the Union, that great palladium of our liberty and safety, the least irreverently spoken of. Our citizenship in the United States is our national character, our citizenship in any particular State is only our local distinction. Our great title is *Americans*, our inferior one varies with the place." —(*Thomas Paine, the Crisis, No.* XV.)

W. H. BARTLETT,

In his "History of the United States of America," says:

"It was at this critical period, while this feeling, though inoperative, yet lingered in the minds of the people, and when, although the thing itself had become familiarized to most minds as equally necessary and desirable, every one held back from boldly pronouncing the word INDEPENDENCE, that there appeared a pamphlet called 'Common Sense,' written by Thomas Paine, the celebrated author of the 'Rights of Man,' who had recently emigrated from England, and ardently embraced the American cause. Perceiving the hesitation in the public mind, he set himself to the work of dissipating it by a clear and convincing statement of the actual position of affairs. He plainly exposed the impossibility of a lasting reconciliation with England, and showed that independence had not only become the only safe or honorable course, but that it was as practicable as it was desirable. * * * * This pamphlet, written in a popular and convincing style, and expressly adapted to the state of public feeling, produced an indescribable sensation. The ice was now broken; those who,

although convinced, had hitherto held back, came boldly
forward, while many who had halted between two opinions now yielded to the force of necessity and embraced the popular side."

"It is only by acting in union that the usurpations of foreign
nations on the freedom of trade can be counteracted, and security
extended to the commerce of America. And when we view a flag,
which, to the eye, is beautiful, and to contemplate its rise and
origin, inspires a sensation of sublime delight, our national honor
must unite with our interest to prevent injury to the one, or insult
to the other."—(*Thomas Paine*, "*The Crisis*," *No.* XVI.)

DR. JOHN W. FRANCIS,

Of New York, said:

"No work had the demand for readers comparable to
that of Paine. 'The Age of Reason' on its first appearance in New York was printed as an orthodox book, by
orthodox publishers, doubtless deceived by the vast re-
nown which the author of 'Common Sense' had obtained."

"His (Paine's) career was wonderful, even for the
age of miraculous events he lived in. In America he
was a revolutionary hero of the first rank, who carried
letters in his pocket from George Washington thanking
him for his services; and he managed besides to write
his name in large letters in the history of England and
France."—(*Atlantic Monthly, vol.* iv, *p.* 16.)

"The Democratic movement of the last eighty years,
be it a 'finality' or only a phase of progress towards a
more perfect state, is the grand historical fact of modern
times, and Paine's name is intimately connected with
it."—(*Ibid, p.* 17.)

BÈNJ. F. LOSSING

Says: "It (Common Sense) was the earliest and most powerful appeal in behalf of independence, and probably did more to fix that idea firmly in the public mind than any other instrumentality."—(*Field Book of Revolution, vol.* ii, *p.* 274.)

"The flame of desire for absolute independence glowed in every patriot bosom at the beginning of 1776, and the vigorous paragraphs of 'Common Sense,' and kindred publications, laboring with the voice of impassioned oratory at every public gathering of the people, uncapped the volcano."—(*Ibid, p.* 277.)

"It is only in the creation that all our ideas and conceptions of a word of God can unite. The creation speaketh a universal language, independently of human speech, or human language, multiplied and various as they be. It is an ever existing original which every man can read. It cannot be forged; it cannot be counterfeited; it cannot be lost; it cannot be altered; it cannot be suppressed. It does not depend upon the will of man whether it shall be published or not; it publishes itself from one end of the earth to the other. It preaches to all nations and to all worlds, and this word of God reveals to man all that is necessary for man to know of God. Do we want to contemplate his power? We see it in the immensity of the creation. Do we want to contemplate his wisdom? We see it in the unchangeable order by which the incomprehensible whole is governed. Do we want to contemplate his munificence? We see it in the abundance with which he fills the earth. Do we want to contemplate his mercy? We see it in his not withholding that abundance even from the unthankful."— (*Paine's "Age of Reason," page* 26.)

DR. LADD,

A prominent poet of the Revolution, and, of course, like Ramsay, Allen, Botta, Gordon, and others, cited in this

4*

little work, a cotemporary of Thomas. Paine, pays the
following eloquent and glowing tribute to that remarkable man :

> " Long live the man, in early contest found,
>   Who spoke his heart when dastards trembled round;
>   Who, fired with more than Greek or Roman rage,
>   Flashed truth on tyrants from his manly page—
>   Immortal Paine! whose pen surprised we saw,
>   Could fashion Empires while it kindled awe.
>   When first with awful front to crush her foes,
>   All bright in glittering arms, Columbia rose,
>   From thee our sons the generous mandate took,
>   As if from Heaven some oracle had spoke ;
>   And when thy pen revealed the grand design,
>   *'Twas done*—Columbia's liberty was thine."

" It is certain that, in one point, all nations of the earth and all
religions agree; all believe in a God; the things in which they dis-
agree are the redundancies annexed to that belief; and, therefore,
if ever an universal religion should prevail, it will not be believing
anything new, but getting rid of redundancies, and believing as
man first believed. Adam, if ever there was such a man, was
created a Deist; but in the meantime let every man follow, as he
has a right to do, the religion and worship he prefers."—(*Age of
Reason, p.* 58.)

JAMES CHEETHAM,

The notorious apostate, speaking of whose "Life of
Paine," a Christian cotemporary* of his remarked, "*we
have every reason to believe* IT IS A LIBEL ALMOST FROM
BEGINNING TO END," is compelled to admit, speaking of
Paine's 'Common Sense,' that: (See "Life of Paine," pp.
45-6.)

---

* Solomon Southwick.

"This pamphlet, of 40 octavo pages, holding out re-lief by proposing INDEPENDENCE to an oppressed and despairing people, was published in January, 1776. Speaking a language which the Colonists had felt but not thought, its popularity, terrible in its consequences to the parent country, was unexampled in the history of the press. At first, involving the Colonists, it was thought, in the crime of rebellion, and pointing to a road leading inevitably to ruin, it was read with indig-nation and alarm, but when the reader, (and everybody read it) recovering from the first shock, reperused it, its arguments, nourishing his feelings and appealing to his pride, re-animated his hopes and satisfied his under-standing, that 'Common Sense,' backed by the resources and forces of the Colonies, poor and feeble as they were, could alone rescue them from the unqualified oppression with which they were threatened." "His pen was an appendage to the army of Independence as necessary and as formidable as its cannon. Having no property he fared as the army fared. * * * When the Colo-nists drooped, he revived them with a 'Crisis.' The object of it was good, the method excellent, and the language suited to the depressed spirits of the army." —(*Life of Paine, page* 55.)

JAMES THOMPSON CALLENDER,

In his "Sketches of the History of America," says: (1798.)

"On *titles* Thomas Paine has written with great suc-cess; and this is one reason why the friends of order hate him. Abuse of this author is now as naturally expected in a federal newspaper as tea and chocolate in a grocer's store. To such things compare two resolutions of Congress of the 26th August, and 3d October, 1785. In consequence of his 'early, unsolicited, and continued labors in explaining and enforcing the principles of the late Revolution, by ingenious and timely publications, upon the nature of liberty and civil government,' they direct the board of treasury to pay him three thousand dollars. This attestation outweighs the clamor of the six per cent. orators. They dread, they revile, and, if able, they would persecute Thomas Paine, because he possesses talents and courage sufficient to rend assunder the mantle of speculation, and to delineate the rickety growth of our public debt."

* * * * "Wishing ye may always fully and uninterruptedly enjoy every civil and religious right; and be in your turn the means of securing it to others, but that the example which ye have unwisely set, of mingling religion with politics, *may be disavowed and reprobated by* EVERY *inhabitant of America* "—(*Paine's "Address to Quakers."*)

CHARLES BOTTA,

An Italian patriot, historian, and physician, who fought for American Independence, and who must have been a good judge of the influence and merits of Paine's writings, says:

"At this epoch appeared a writing entitled 'Common Sense;' it was the production of Thomas Paine, born in England, and arrived not long before in America. No writer, perhaps, ever possessed, in a higher degree, the art of moving and guiding the multitude at his will. It may be affirmed, in effect, that this work was one of the most powerful instruments of American Independence. The author endeavored, with very plausible arguments, to demonstrate that the opposition of parties, the diversity of interests, the arrogance of the British Government, and its ardent thirst of vengeance, rendered all reconciliation impossible. On the other hand, he enlarged upon the necessity, utility, and possibility of Independence. * * * The success of this writing of Paine cannot be described."

"O! ye that love mankind! ye that dare oppose, not only the tyranny, but the tyrant, stand forth! Every spot in the old world is overrun with oppression. Freedom hath been hunted round the Globe, Asia and Africa have long expelled her. Europe regards her like a stranger, and England hath given her warning to depart. O! receive the fugitive, and prepare in time an asylum for mankind."—(*Paine's* "*Common Sense.*")

THOMAS GASPEY,

In his "History of England," says:

"At this period the celebrated Thomas Paine had entered upon his career as a public writer. In January, 1776, his pamphlet, entitled 'Common Sense,' appeared. That able production has been said to have been the joint composition of Paine, Dr. Franklin, Mr. Samuel and John Adams. Paine, however, denies that they in any way directly assisted him; to the two latter gentlemen he was not known at the time. He had been introduced to Franklin in England. * * * * * Paine was originally a member of the Society of Friends, and brought up as a staymaker at Thetford. Subsequently he obtained a situation in the excise, but left it to become an assistant in a school; he became an exciseman again, and a pamphlet which he wrote caused him to be noticed by Franklin, who advised him to visit America. 'Common Sense' opened with reflections on the origin and design of government, and it then proceeded with a vigorous hand to expose the abuses which had crept into the English system. * * * * The clear and powerful style of Paine made a prodigious impression on the American people. * * * * * He was treated with great consideration by the members of the Revolutionary Government, *who took no step of importance without consulting him.*"

"The world may know, that as far as we approve of monarchy, *in America the law is king.*"—(*Common Sense, p.* 46.)

STEPHEN SIMPSON,

Author of a "Life of Stephen Girard," &c., says, in his "Lives of Washington and Jefferson with a Parallel:"

"To these followed pamphlets and essays; among which stood in bold and prominent relief, distinguished for its eloquence, patriotism, and energy, the 'Common Sense' of Thomas Paine; which, combining great force of language, and power of argument with an irresistible array of facts and principles, too obvious to be denied and too reasonable to be confuted, carried conviction to every mind at the same time that they enlisted the most ardent feelings in the cause of liberty and independence; agitating the calm and temperate with a glowing love of country, and infusing irresistible enthusiasm into the bosoms of the ardent champions of the 'Rights of Man.' * * * Lucid in his style, forcible in his diction, and happy in his illustrations, he threw the charms of poetry over the statue of reason, and made converts to liberty as if a power of fascination presided over his pen. * * * The writings of Thomas Paine have been admitted to have had more influence in the accomplishment of the separation of the Colonies from the Mother Country than any other cause. * * To the genius of Thomas Paine, as a popular writer, and to that of George Washington, as a prudent, skillful, and consummate general, are the American people indebted for their rights, liberties and independence. The high opinion of Paine, entertained by Washington, and publicly expressed by the latter, sheds fresh lustre on the incomparable merits of the great leader of the Army of the Revolution."

BAINES, THE HISTORIAN,

In his "Wars of the Revolution," says, speaking of the influence of Paine's political writings in England:

"As the current of popular opinion did not flow in the same direction as the favor of the Court, a pamphlet, entitled the 'Rights of Man,' in which sentiments of an opposite kind were maintained with peculiar asperity and animadversion, was read and circulated in such a manner as to alarm the administration. Editions were multiplied in every form and size; it was alike seen in the hands of the noble and of the plebeian, and became, at length, translated into the various languages of Europe. The cabinet council soon after issued a proclamation against 'wicked and seditious libels,' prosecutions were commenced with a zeal unknown under the government of the reigning family; and it was reserved for the singular fortune of an unlettered man, after contributing by one publication to the establishment of a transatlantic republic in North America, to introduce, with astonishing effect, the doctrines of democratic government into the first states of Europe."

HENRY G. WATSON,

In his "History of the United States," says:

"A pamphlet, entitled 'Common Sense,' written by Thomas Paine, arguing, in plain language, the advantage and necessity of Independence, effected a complete revolution in the feelings and sentiments of the great mass of the people."

"The Almighty Lecturer, by displaying the principles of science in the structure of the universe, has invited man to study and to imitation. It is as if He had said to the inhabitants of this globe, that we call ours, 'I have made an earth for man to dwell upon, and I have rendered the starry heavens visible to teach him science and the arts. He can now provide for his own comfort, AND LEARN FROM MY MUNIFICENCE TO ALL TO BE KIND TO EACH OTHER.' "—(*Paine's* "*Age of Reason,*" p. 33.)

FRANCIS OLDYS, (George Chalmers,)

In his "Life of Paine," says:

"Notwithstanding the reviews of criticism, our author received the applause of party. Nay, Philology came, in the person of Horne Tooke, who found out his retreat after some enquiry, to mingle her cordial congratulations with the thanks of greater powers. '*You are,*' said he, '*like Jove, coming down upon us in a shower of gold.*'"

"If there is a sin superior to every other, it is that of wilful and offensive war. Most other sins are circumscribed within various limits, that is, the power of *one* man cannot give them a very general extension, but he who is the author of war, lets loose the whole contagion of hell, and opens a vein that bleeds a nation to death."—("*The Crisis,*" No. 5.)

CAPEL LOFFT,

An English barrister, poet and miscellaneous writer, made use of the following language, in a letter to T. C. Rickman, in 1795, after strongly criticising the "Age of Reason:"

"I am glad Paine is living: he cannot be even wrong without enlightening mankind; such is the vigor of his intellect, such the acuteness of his research, and such the force and vivid perspicuity of his expression."

ALEXANDER ANDREWS,

In his "History of British Journalism," says:

"Soon after this Thomas Paine's pamphlet, published at irregular periods, but all numbered and paged like newspapers, and named the 'American Crisis,' appeared, and first pronounced the words which had been faltering upon so many blanched lips, and trembling tongues of men who shuddered as they saw the only alternative more plainly—Independence and Separation."

* * * * "In my religious publications my endeavors have been directed to bring man to a right use of the reason that God has given him; to impress on him the great principles of divine morality, justice, mercy, and a benevolent disposition to all men, and to all creatures, and to inspire in him a spirit of trust, confidence, and consolation in his Creator, unshackled by the fables of books pretending to be the word of God."—(*Thomas Paine.*)

MR. BOND,

An English Surgeon, who was confined in the Luxembourg prison in Paris at the same time Paine was, and
5

who disagreed with him in both political and theological matters, asserts that:

"Mr Paine, while hourly expecting to die, read to me parts of his 'Age of Reason,' and every night when I left him to be separately locked up, and expected not to see him alive in the morning, he always expressed his firm belief in the principles of that book, and begged I would tell the world such were his dying opinions. He often said that if he lived he should prosecute further that work and print it."

Mr. Bond has frequently observed, says Rickman, the poet, that Paine was—

"The most conscientious man he ever knew."

"My path is a right line, as straight and clear to me as a ray of light. The boldness (if they will have it so) with which I speak on any subject, is a compliment to the person I address; it is like saying to him, I treat you as a man, and not as a child. With respect to any worldly object, as it is impossible to discover any in me, therefore what I do, and my manner of doing it, ought to be ascribed to a good motive."—(*Thomas Paine*)

WILLIAM SMYTHE,

In his "Lectures on Modern History," speaking of the "American Revolution," says:

"You will now observe the arguments that were used; you will see them in the very celebrated pamphlet of Paine—his 'Common Sense'—a pamphlet whose effect was such that it was quite a feature in this memorable contest. You may now read it, and wonder how a performance not marked, as you may at first sight suppose, with any particular powers of eloquence could possibly produce effects so striking. * * * * The pamphlet of Paine was universally read and admired in America, and is said to have contributed most materially to the vote of Independence, passed by Congress in 1776."

REV. ABIEL HOLMES,

In his "Annals of America," says:

"A pamphlet, under the signature of 'Common Sense,' written by Thomas Paine, produced great effect. While it demonstrated the necessity, the advantages, and the practicability of Independence, it treated kingly government with opprobrium, and hereditary succession with ridicule. The change of the public mind on this occasion is without a parallel."

GUILLAUME TELL POUSSIN,

In his work entitled "The United States; its Power and Progress," says of the influence of Paine's writings :

"The condition of affairs day by day assumed a graver aspect. The unequal struggle between England and the still growing Colonies gave a decided preponderance to ideas of Independence. Several remarkable productions seemed to favor this enthusiasm. That of Thomas Paine, entitled 'Common Sense,' exerted an overpowering influence. It rendered the sentiment of Independence national; and Congress, being the organ of public opinion, soon prepared to adopt this sentiment. By the resolution of the 8th of May, 1776, each Colony was requested to reject all authority emanating from the British Crown, and to establish a form of government that would accord with the particular interest of each State, and with that of the whole Confederation."

"Paine also wrote a series of political pamphlets called 'The Crisis,' which were admirably adapted to the state of the times, and which did much toward keeping alive the spirit of determined rebellion against the unjust government of Great Britain."—*Benjamin F. Lossing, in his Field Book of the Revolution, Vol. II, page 274, Note.*

APPLETON'S CYCLOPÆDIA OF BIOGRAPHY

Says:

"He (Paine) then published his celebrated pamphlet, 'Common Sense,' which, being written with great vigor and addressed to a highly excited population, had a prodigious sale, and undoubtedly accelerated the famous Declaration of Independence. * * *. * He arrived in Calais, in September, 1792. The garrison at Calais were under arms to receive this 'friend of liberty,' the tri-colored cockade was presented to him by the mayor, and the handsomest woman in the town was selected to place it in his hat. Meantime Paine had been declared in Paris worthy of the honors of citizenship, and he proceeded thither, where he was received with every demonstration of extravagant joy."

"Washington's retreat to Trenton was a compulsive one. * * * I do not believe *that even a number of 'The Crisis' could have saved the American army* and cause from annihilation, if Howe had been an active and persevering, an enlightened and energetic commander."—(*Cheetham's Life of Paine, p. 57.*)

"The last 'Crisis' was published in Philadelphia April 19th, 1783. Peace was now substantially concluded, and the Independence of the United States acknowledged. He *who, if not the suggester, was the ablest literary advocate of independence,* could do no less, when independence was acquired, than salute the nation on the great event."—(*Ibid, p. 92.*)

JOHN FROST, LL. D.,

In his History of the United States, says:

"During the winter of 1775–6, many of the most able writers in America were employed in demonstrating the necessity and propriety of a total separation from the mother country, and the establishment of constitutional governments in the Colonies. One of the most conspicuous of these writers was Thomas Paine, who published a pamphlet under the signature of 'Common Sense,' which produced great effect. It demonstrated the necessity, advantages and practicability of independence, and heaped reproach and disgrace on monarchial governments, and ridicule on hereditary succession. * * * * * Paine had shrewdness and cunning mixed with boldness in his manner of writing, and to this, perhaps, may be ascribed the uncommon effect of his essays on the inflamed minds of the Americans.— (*History U. S., vol.* I, *pp.* 192–3, *Simeon Collins, Philadelphia,* 1844.)

"Let men learn to feel that the true greatness of a nation is founded on the principles of humanity; and that to avoid a war when her own existence is not endangered, and wherein the happiness of man must be wantonly sacrificed, is a higher principle of true honor than madly to engage in it."—(*Paine in "Prospects on the Rubicon."*)

The author of "The Religion of Science," in his introduction to his Life of Paine, published by Calvin Blanchard, of New York, says:

"There needs but to have the light of truth shine fully upon the real character of Thomas Paine, to prove him to have been a far greater man than his most ardent admirers have hitherto given him credit for being."

5*

HENRY S. RANDALL,

In his "Life of Jefferson," says:

" We confess we have no sympathy with Mr. Paine's religious views. If his personal character was what it is commonly alleged to have been, (though it is now said there has been a good deal of exaggeration, *and even out and out invention* on this head,) there was much in it no man can admire. But concede all the allegations against him, and it still leaves him the author of 'Common Sense,' and certain other papers, which rung like clarions in the darkest hour of the Revolutionary struggle, inspiring the bleeding, and starving, and pestilence-stricken, as the pen of no other man ever inspired them. Whatever Paine's faults or vices, however dark and crapulous the close of his stormy career, when he is spoken of as the patriot, and especially as the Revolutionary and *pre-Revolutionary* writer, *shame rest on the pen which dares not do him justice!* and shame, also, ought to rest on the most cursory narrator of the events which heralded the Declaration of Independence, who should omit to enumerate the publication of 'Common Sense' among them."

THE NEW YORK ADVERTISER,

Of June 9th, 1809, has the following notice:

" Mr. Thomas Paine.—

" 'Thy spirit, Independence, let me share.'—*Smollett.*

"With heartfelt sorrow and poignant regret we are compelled to announce to the world that Mr. Thomas Paine is no more. This distinguished philanthropist, whose life was devoted to the cause of humanity, departed this life yesterday morning, and if any man's

memory deserved a place in the breast of a freeman, it
is that of the deceased, for

> " 'Take him, for all in all,
>   We ne'er shall look upon his like again.'

"The friends of the deceased are invited to attend his
funeral by 9 o'clock in the morning, from his late resi-
dence at Greenwich, from whence his corpse will be
conveyed to New Rochelle, for interment.

> " 'His ashes there,
>   His fame every where.' "

"Every government that does not act on the principle of a republic, or, in other words, does not make the *res-publica* its whole
and sole object, is not a good government. Republican government is no other than government established and conducted
for the interest of the public, as well individually as collectively.
It is not necessarily connected with any particular form, but it
most naturally associates with the representative form as being the
best calculated to secure the end for which a nation is at the expense
of supporting it."—(" *Rights of Man*," *Mendum's Complete Ed.*,
Vol. II, *page* 172.)

The UNIVERSAL MAGAZINE and REVIEW

For April, 1793, concludes a review of "The Rights of
Man" with these words:

"And now, courteous reader, we leave Mr. Paine
entirely to thy mercy; what wilt thou say of him?
Wilt thou address him? 'Thou art a troubler of privi-
leged orders—we will tar and feather thee; nobles
abhor thee, and kings think thee mad!' Or wilt thou
rather put on thy spectacles, study Mr. Paine's physi-
ognomy, purchase his print, hang it over thy chimney
piece and, pointing to it, say: '*this is no common man;
this is* THE POOR MAN'S FRIEND!'"

WATSON,

In his "Annals of Philadelphia," says:

"In June, 1785, John Fitch called on the ingenious William Henry, Esq., of Lancaster, to take his opinion of his draughts, who informed him that he (Fitch) was not the the *first* person who had thought of applying steam to vessels, for that Thomas Paine, author of 'Common Sense' had suggested the same to him, (Henry) in the winter of 1778."

"There is a single idea, which, if it strikes rightly on the mind, either in a legal or a religious sense, will prevent any man, or any body of men, or any government, from going wrong on the subject of religion; which is, that before any human institutions of government were known in the world, there existed, if I may so express it, a compact between God and man, from the beginning of time: and that as the relation and condition which man in his individual person stands in towards his Maker cannot be changed by any human laws or human authority, that religious devotion, which is a part of this compact, cannot so much as be made a subject of human laws; and that all laws must conform themselves to this prior existing compact, and not assume to make the compact conform to the laws, which, besides being human, are subsequent thereunto. The first act of man, when he looked around and saw himself a creature which he did not make, and a world furnished for his reception, must have been devotion; and devotion must ever continue sacred to every individual man, as it appears right to him; and governments do mischief by interfering."—*Thos. Paine.* (*See works vol. 2, page 114, Boston Edition,* 1856.)

THE AUTHOR OF "THE ANALYST,"

Published by Wiley & Putnam, New York, 1840, says of Paine:

"It is allowed by all liberal judges, that, in his 'Common Sense' and 'The Crisis,' he strengthened in the American mind its aspirations after liberty; gave them tho right direction, *manfully exhorted them in their waver-ing hour; and acted the part of a freeman and an active friend to humanity."*

WALTER MORTON,

In a short narrative of Paine, says:

"In his religious opinions he continued to the last as steadfast and tenacious as any sectarian to the definition of his own creed. He never, indeed, broached the sub-ject first, but to intrusive and inquisitive visitors, who came to try him on that point, his general answer was to this effect: 'My opinions are now before the world, and all have an opportunity to refute them if they can. *I* believe them unanswerable truths, and that I have done great service to mankind by boldly putting them forth. I do not wish to argue upon the subject now. I have labored disinterestedly in the cause of truth.' I shook his hand after his use of speech was gone; but, while the other organs told me sufficiently that he knew me and appreciated my affection, his eye glistened with genius under the pangs of death."

THE GENERAL ASSEMBLY OF PENN'A,

In 1785, passed the following:

"*Whereas,* During the late Revolution, and particularly in the most trying and perilous times thereof, many very eminent services were rendered to the people of the United States by Thomas Paine, Esq., accompanied with sundry distinguished instances of *fidelity, patriot-ism and disinterestedness;*

"*And whereas,* That the said Thomas Paine did, du-ring the whole progress of the Revolution, *voluntarily devote himself* to the service of the public, *without accept-ing recompense* therefor, and, moreover did decline taking or receiving the profits which authors are entitled to on the sale of their literary works, but relinquished them for the better accommodation of the country, and for the honor of the public cause;

"*And whereas,* Besides the knowledge which this House has of the services of the said Thomas Paine, the same having been recommended to us by his Excellency, the President, and the Supreme Executive Council of the State, of the 16th of December last past, and by the friendly offices of the late patriotic Commander-in-chief, General Washington;

"*Be it enacted,* And it is hereby enacted, by the Representatives of the freemen of the Commonwealth of Pennsylvania, in General Assembly met, and by the authority of the same, that, as a temporary recompense the said Thomas Paine, and until a suitable provision shall be further made, either federally by Congress, or otherwise, the Supreme Executive Council be authorized and empowered to draw on the Treasurer of this State for the sum of £500 in favor of and payable to the said Thomas Paine.

"Signed by order of the House,

"JOHN BAYARD, *Speaker.*"

The following song, though the same metre as the "Star Spangled Banner," was written by Mr. Paine, many years before the production of our national song by Mr. Key, and was originally published under the title of

"THE BOSTON PATRIOTIC SONG."

Ye sons of Columbia who bravely have fought
For those rights which unstain'd from your sires have descended,
May you long taste the blessings your valor has bought,
And your sons reap the soil which your fathers defended;
Mid the reign of mild peace

May your nation increase
With the glory of Rome, and the wisdom of Greece;
And ne'er may the sons of Columbia be slaves
While the earth bears a plant or the sea rolls its waves.

The fame of our arms, of our laws the mild sway,
  Had justly ennobled our nation in story,
'Till the dark clouds of faction obscured our bright day
  And envelop'd the sun of American glory; -
      But let traitors be told,
      Who their country have sold,
    And bartered their God for his image in gold,
      That ne'er shall the sons, &c.

While France her huge limbs bathes recumbent in blood,
  And society's base, threats with wide dissolution;
May peace like the dove, who returned from the flood,
  Find an ark of abode in our mild constitution;
      But though peace is our aim,
      Yet the boon we disclaim
    If bought by our sovereignty, justice or fame.
      For ne'er shall the sons, &c.

'Tis the fire of the flint each American warms,
  Let Rome's haughty victors beware of collision!
Let them bring all the vassals of Europe in arms,
  We're a world by ourselves, and disdain a division;
      While with patriot pride
      To our laws we're allied,
    No foe can subdue us, no faction divide;
      For ne'er shall the sons, &c.

Let our patriots destroy vile anarchy's worm,
  Lest our liberty's growth should be check'd by corrosion,
Then let clouds thicken round us, we heed not the storm,
  Our earth fears no shock, but the earth's own explosion.
      Foes assail us in vain,
      Tho' their fleets bridge the main,
    For our altars and claims, with our lives we'll mantain.
      For ne'er shall the sons, &c.

Let Fame, to the world, sound America's voice,
  No intrigue can her sons from their government sever;

Its wise regulations and laws, are *their* choice,
And shall flourish till Liberty slumber forever.
Then unite heart and hand,
Like Leonidas' band;
And swear by the God of the ocean and land,
That ne'er shall the sons of Columbia be slaves,
While the earth bears a plant, or the sea rolls its waves.

GEORGE JACOB HOLYOAKE,

Author of "The Trial of Theism," &c., and editor of "The London Reasoner," says:

"Paine, like Defoe, was the personation of English common sense. * * * * Paine was the Prophet of American Destiny—the great Pamphleteer of its Independence. * * * He was the Thinker for the People. He found out the obvious thoughts of the period and showed them to the nation, and created those which were wanting. * * * * Paine's merits and demerits were all popular. His errors were broad and his virtues hearty. There was nothing small or mean about him. He was a strong man all through. The man who was the confidant of Burke, (before the unhappy days when Burke's reason failed him,) the counsellor of Franklin, and the friend and colleague of Washington, must have had great qualities. * * * * If Paine was coarse, he had capacity and integrity; if the oak was gnarled, it had strength—if the ore was rough, there was gold in it. * * * * Let us do justice to him."

ERRATA.

Page 7, Washington, line 13, read *epocha* for epoch.
Page 8, Adams, line 10, read *attempts* for attempt.
Page 12, Southwick, dele *Rev.*
Page 12,   "   line 3, read *Visitant* for Visiter.
Page 12,   "   line 9, read *Tyrtæus* for Tintochus.

www.ingramcontent.com/pod-product-compliance
Lightning Source LLC
Chambersburg PA
CBHW021633270326
41931CB00008B/996